DODD, MEAD WONDERS BOOKS include WONDERS OF:

ALLIGATORS AND CROCODILES.
  Blassingame
ANIMAL NURSERIES. Berrill
BARNACLES. Ross and Emerson
BAT WORLD. Lavine
BEYOND THE SOLAR SYSTEM.
  Feravolo
BISON WORLD. Lavine and Scuro
CACTUS WORLD. Lavine
CARIBOU. Rearden
DINOSAUR WORLD. Matthews
DONKEYS. Lavine and Scuro
EAGLE WORLD. Lavine
FLY WORLD. Lavine
FROGS AND TOADS. Blassingame
GEESE AND SWANS. Fegely
GEMS. Pearl
GRAVITY. Feravolo
HAWK WORLD. Lavine
HERBS. Lavine
HUMMINGBIRDS. Simon
JELLYFISH. Jacobson and Franz
KELP FOREST. Brown
LLAMAS. Perry
LIONS. Schaller
MARSUPIALS. Lavine
MEASUREMENT. Lieberg
MONKEY WORLD. Berrill

MOSQUITO WORLD. Ault
OWL WORLD. Lavine
PELICAN WORLD. Cook and Schreiber
PRAIRIE DOGS. Chace
PRONGHORN. Chace
RACCOONS. Blassingame
ROCKS AND MINERALS. Pearl
SEA GULLS. Schreiber
SEALS AND SEA LIONS. Brown
SPIDER WORLD. Lavine
SPONGES. Jacobson and Pang
STARFISH. Jacobson and Emerson
STORKS. Kahl
TERNS. Schreiber
TERRARIUMS. Lavine
TREE WORLD. Cosgrove
TURTLE WORLD. Blassingame
WILD DUCKS. Fegely
WOODS AND DESERT AT NIGHT.
  Berrill
WORLD OF THE ALBATROSS. Fisher
WORLD OF BEARS. Bailey
WORLD OF HORSES. Lavine and
  Casey
WORLD OF SHELLS. Jacobson and
  Emerson
WORLD OF WOLVES. Berrill
YOUR SENSES. Cosgrove

WONDERS OF MARSUPIALS

Sigmund A. Lavine

Illustrated with photographs and old prints

DODD, MEAD & COMPANY · NEW YORK

Illustrations courtesy of: Australian Information Service, 10, 36, 40, 41, 42, 44, 46, 48, 50, 54, 56, 58, 60, 62, 64, 65, 67, 69, 70, 72, 73, 74, 76; Dorothy M. Bryan, 53; New York Zoological Society, 26; Queensland Government Tourist Bureau, 51; U.S. Fish and Wildlife Service, Frank L. Blake, *frontispiece*, 7; Virginia Commission of Game and Inland Fisheries, L. G. Kesteloo, 18, 24; Zoologcal Society of London, 28, 30.

1 2 3 4 5 6 7 8 9 10

Library of Congress Cataloging in Publication Data

Lavine, Sigmund A
  Wonders of marsupials.

  Includes index.
  SUMMARY: Discusses some of the 248 species
of marsupials.
  1. Marsupialia—Juvenile literature. [1. Marsupials]
I. Title.
QL737.M3L33   599'.2   78-7745
ISBN 0-396-07619-X

FOR HARRIET—
    who is thankful all sons do not
    take after their fathers

Contents

WONDERS OF MARSUPIALS

Note the long, tapering, white-tipped prehensile tail on this ring-tailed possum. It is used to hold onto branches and as an extra finger.

1. Meet the Marsupials

"Nature does nothing without a purpose."

Marsupials are pouched animals—meaning that the females carry their young in pouches. These can be big, elastic, fur-lined bags—kangaroos have the largest pouches of any marsupials— or they can be shallow; or they can open downward and slightly backward. Some marsupials have undeveloped pouches composed of two flaps of skin. But the flaps, like the pouches, regardless of size and shape, surround the nipples. The number of nipples varies from two to twenty-seven, depending on the species.

Why a Pouch?

The physical characteristic of having a pouch is the source of the word "marsupial." Scientists coined it from the Latin *marsupium* (pouch).

The purpose of the pouch is to provide the young with protection. They need it. Newly born marsupials are extremely tiny and only partially developed. The common opossum of the Americas, which is about the size of a house cat when fully grown, is only as big as a bee at birth. The gray kangaroo, which may be six feet tall at maturity, is an inch long when born.

Besides being tiny, infant marsupials are blind, hairless, and lack fully developed hind legs. But the forelimbs are relatively large and are equipped with sharp claws. Immediately after birth, the baby, using its front legs and claws, crawls through the fur on its mother's stomach to the pouch, which holds the youngster close to the nipples. Here it remains until it is able to fend for itself—which may take as long as eight months.

Once in the pouch a young marsupial attaches itself firmly to a nipple. The nipple then swells to such a size that it is impossible to detach the baby from it without rupturing the sides of the mouth. Meanwhile, the youngster's windpipe lengthens and tilts upward and forward so that it fits into the rear of the nasal tunnel. This not only prevents milk from getting into the windpipe but also permits air to be delivered directly to the lungs. As a result, the baby can breathe while suckling. Because marsupial young are too helpless to nurse, milk is squirted into their mouths by periodic contractions of muscles above the mother's nipples.

Cradled in the pouch, the baby is transported by the female as she goes about her usual activities. Female marsupials lacking pouches also carry their offspring everywhere they go. At birth, their young clamp their mouths on a nipple which swells and becomes so firmly fastened in the mouth that the baby cannot lose its grip. To keep the infant from dragging on the ground, the female elevates her hindquarters by arching her back.

In the beginning

Most animals differ from their original ancestors. But the marsupials are "living fossils." They have undergone little change in at least a hundred million years. For example: the ten-foot tall kangaroo that hopped across Australia some two million years ago looked exactly like its present-day descendants except for its size.

The kangaroo is still the largest marsupial although the ten-foot tall prehistoric "monster" has vanished.

Although fossils reveal much about marsupials, we lack a complete record of their early history. Most zoologists believe that pouched animals and the placentals—animals whose young receive nourishment from their mother's blood until born—had a common ancestry. But the two groups soon diverged and evolved in different directions.

Over the centuries the placentals have developed physical features that have helped them survive. These intelligent animals also have adapted to varying environments and climates. But the majority of the marsupials have been unable to adjust to changing conditions.

As a result, the ten-foot tall kangaroo vanished along with other marsupial "monsters." Gone is the pouched lion, marsupial saber-toothed cats, and *Diprotodon*, largest of all pouched animals. *Diprotodon* was as big as a rhinoceros and "looked like a nightmare rabbit."

Not only have large marsupials become extinct but so have numerous normal-sized species. For example, eons ago when South America was isolated by the sea, the continent provided habitats for many species of pouched animals. Today, the only marsupials in South America are several species of opossums and a group of small rodent-like creatures. All other marsupials disappeared after placental mammals reached South America when land connections with other regions were re-established.

What happened to the marsupials in South America was repeated in many other areas. Eventually, placentals ousted pouched animals from most parts of the world. It was not a difficult task. Once found all over the Earth, marsupials are now confined to North and South America, Australia, and certain islands near the latter continent.

Why they have survived

The opossums of the New World are the exception to the general rule that marsupials cannot adjust to new conditions. The various species of opossums native to North and South America have withstood changes in climate, competition from more advanced animals, and the activities of man. More than merely surviving, some species increase in numbers and extend their range every year. Because all New World opossums have a similar anatomical structure, zoologists have grouped them in a single family, but they differ greatly in size, coloration, shape, and habits.

Number please?

Scientists have classified 248 species of marsupials. Seventy-two, 65 of them opossums, are native to the Americas while the great majority—176 species—inhabit the Australasian region.

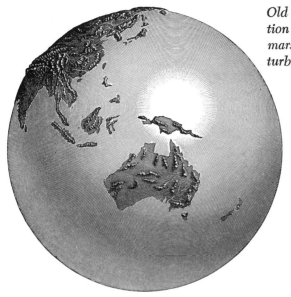

Old map shows the isolation of Australia where marsupials lived undisturbed by placentals.

30 Australia

BRUSHTAIL POSSUM
R BATES   R S A

Some of Australia's many marsupials are depicted on stamps.

As indicated, the marsupials of North America are mostly opossums but in Australasia the marsupials differ greatly in behavior, and range in size from the red kangaroo whose tail is nearly four feet long to minute mice no bigger than grasshoppers.

Some Australasian marsupials resemble various placental mammals (as did certain extinct pouched animals). Not only do these marsupials have many of the anatomical features of the animals they duplicate but also their actions are the same. Zoologists call this development of similar characteristics in unrelated forms "convergence."

The placentals and their "look alikes" occupy the same niches in nature. Thus, although Australia has no flying squirrels,

15

groundhogs, or wolves, their places are filled by flying phalangers, wombats, and the Tasmanian wolf. Meanwhile, the destructive mice and jerboas found in other parts of the world are replaced in Australia by tiny pouched mice.

Because the marsupials of Australasia cannot cope with the inroads of civilization or with placental animals, they have survived only because the island continent and the surrounding lands have been separated from the rest of the world for a very long time. Indeed, it well may be that in the future most species of pouched animals native to Australasia will be extinct except for specimens living in sanctuaries and in zoos. This is because man has introduced animals into the marsupials' habitat that compete with them for food, water, and shelter.

If the marsupials native to Australasia had the amazing powers of survival of the New World marsupials, the task of conservationists "Down Under" would be far easier.

2. New World Marsupials

"Here come . . . some very strange beasts."

King Ferdinand and Queen Isabella stared at the strange animal Vincent Pinzon had brought back from the coast of Brazil in A.D. 1500. As Their Royal Highnesses examined the strange creature—the first marsupial to be exhibited in Europe—a scribe recorded that it had the face of a fox, tail of a monkey, ears like a bat, and human hands. The scribe also noted that the animal had two stomachs, one below the other, and described how the young were carried in the lower stomach. Fascinated by the marsupial pouch, the Spanish called the opossum the "Incredible Mother." This was far more complimentary than the opossum's first scientific name which appeared in Konrad Gessner's *Historiae Animalium*, published in 1558. Gessner called the opossum *simia vulpina*, or "monkey fox."

Because all the females of the opossum species native to the Americas have two wombs, these marsupials are called Didelphids, a word derived from the Greek *di* (double) and *delphys* (womb).

While all Didelphids have the same type of anatomical structure, they differ in size. The smallest is less than three inches

long, the largest is big as a house cat. Nocturnal feeders, Didelphids eat everything that can be digested, from carrion to leaves.

Although the behavior patterns of opossums vary greatly, no Didelphid displays much intelligence. Indeed, the common opossum—commonly called 'possum—is credited with being the stupidest animal in the American woods. Nevertheless, this native of the Argentine has not only flourished for one hundred million years and increased in numbers but also has learned to live in woodlands as far north as lower Canada.

COMMON OPOSSUM

The common opossum's reputation for stupidity is well deserved. For example, if a 'possum is caught in a trap and manages to escape, the chances are it will enter the same trap the following night!

Nevertheless, the dim-witted 'possum is one of the most successful of all animals. Actually, there are three reasons why this slow-moving, awkward, small-brained creature has prospered. First, as indicated, opossums eat anything and everything. Second, they breed regularly. Third, their habit of "playing 'possum" (feigning death) protects them from their enemies.

When an opossum pretends it's dead, its heartbeat slows and it lies passively on its side, mouth open, tongue hanging out, eyes closed. While "dead" an opossum does not stir, even if it is swung by the tail or brutally mauled. At one time it was thought that opossums played dead to make their foes leave them alone. But current thought holds that, when limp and motionless, opossums are actually in a trance induced by fear.

Captain John Smith—the first Englishman to see a Didelphid—wrote the classic description of the common opossum in A.D. 1608: "An Opassom hath an head like a Swine, and a taile

A common opossum

Captain John Smith gave a classic description of the common opossum in 1608.

like a Rat, and is of the bignes of a Cat. Under her belly she hath a bagge, wherein shee lodgeth, carrieth, and sucketh her young."

While Smith is credited with being the first Englishman to describe the opossum the honor does not belong to him. Actually, it should be paid to Thomas Harriot, the scientist who served as geographer during Sir Walter Raleigh's second expedition to Virginia in 1585. But Harriot's description of the opossum is not nearly as colorful as the one set down by naturalist Richard Eden in 1555: "Emonge these trees is fownde that monstrous beaste with a snowte lyke a foxe, a tayle lyke a marmasette, eares lyke a batte, handes lyke a man, and feete lyke an ape, bearing her whelpes abowte with her in an outwarde bellye much lyke unto a greate bagge or purse."

It was far easier for early writers to describe the common opossum than it is for a modern naturalist to do so. The latter knows that opossums differ in appearance throughout their

20

range. The fur, long used to trim inexpensive garments, may vary in color. Opossums in cold regions have thicker white underwool than their southern kin whose fur is also a darker gray. The common opossums of the tropics have very short fur and much longer legs and tails than their relatives in the north. Incidentally, some opossums living in extremely cold regions have exceptionally short ears and tails due to being frostbitten each winter.

All common opossums have the same number of teeth. The mouth (which is larger than man's) contains fifty. This is eight more teeth than either grizzly bears or wolves possess.

Bad-tempered nighttime prowlers, opossums are solitary creatures. As a matter of fact, adults never are seen together, even during the breeding season. Skilled foragers on the ground, opossums have no trouble robbing birds' nests because they are outstanding climbers. Suction pads on the feet and clawed toes enable them to hold tightly to branches. When climbing they use their long, scaly, prehensile tails as another hand or hang by them from a limb. Opossums also coil the tail into a tight hook and use it to carry leaves to their sleeping quarters in hollow trees, abandoned owls' nests, or skunks' dens.

The females give birth to eighteen or more young, each weighing about thirteen-hundredths of a gram. If a newborn human and its mother were in the same proportion to each other as a newborn opossum is to its mother, a six-pound human baby's mother would weigh forty-two tons!

Some members of a litter never enjoy the comforts of their mother's pouch. There are only eleven to thirteen nipples and the youngsters that do not immediately reach and attach to one soon die of starvation.

In ten weeks the survivors are ten times their size at birth. They remain in the pouch for approximately two months. The babies suckle for another thirty days but do not always stay in the pouch. When about the size of a mouse they climb on their

A female common opossum with young

mother's back, entwine their feet and tails in her fur, and are carried about for two months. Once on their own the young opossums separate and lead a hermit's life. Perfectly content, they follow the age-old ways of their kind.

Long before Europeans reached the New World the Indians of North and South America were telling tales and singing songs about the opossum. In the stories told by the tribes that live along the Amazon River, the opossum plays the part of a clever trickster. But in the songs sung by the Seminoles of Florida, the opossum suffers one misfortune after another.

Nor does the 'possum fare very well in the stories told to black children by their slave parents. One of these yarns explains why the opossum's tail is hairless. The story details how Fox, Rabbit, and Opossum decided to steal corn from a field near a graveyard. As they were picking, Opossum saw a ghost coming from the graveyard and started to run away. But just as he was escaping the ghost caught him by the tail and skinned off all the hair. Another tale that was created by black storytellers says that the opossum got its grinning mouth by laughing at other animals.

Perhaps the most outlandish folktale featuring the opossum originated in the swamplands of the Mississippi Delta. It deals with a 'possum that stole the last chicken belonging to a doctor.

The opossum appears in the folklore of tribes living along the Amazon River.

The common opossum is the only marsupial found in North America.

The angry physician shot the thief and prepared the carcass for roasting. But when the oven door was opened, the opossum, which had eaten up all the potatoes and gravy in the pan, ran away unharmed.

There is a grain of truth in this tall tale. Opossums do raid chicken coops. But this is not the main reason southern sportsmen brave the chilly air on nights when the weather is wet and go 'possum hunting. They ignore the dampness—which makes it easy for hunting dogs to pick up an opossum's scent on the moist ground—in hopes of having roast 'possum for Sunday dinner.

When hounds tree a 'possum the hunters do not always shoot it. Some prefer to capture their quarry alive. Usually this is not a difficult task. All they do is shake the branch on which the 'possum sits. When the animal loses its balance and falls, it plays dead and offers no resistance when stuffed into a sack. Incidentally, captured opossums do not make satisfactory pets. Not only do they sleep all day but also they rarely display any affection.

However, penned 'possums that are well fed soon become fat and, when slaughtered, make a very tasty dish. There are almost as many recipes for cooking opossum and sweet potatoes as there are leaves on a persimmon tree—each cook being firmly convinced that his recipe is the best.

Individuals who eat too much 'possum—or anything else—and suffer from indigestion should remember that the Indians claimed an opossum's tail had great medicinal value. Thus it well may be that a stomach pain will vanish at once if the sufferer drinks broth made from a tail. The tail—according to beliefs hundreds of years old—can be compounded into prescriptions that cure colds, clean pores, and "draw out through many applications, any ailment of flesh and bone."

Meanwhile, lexicographers—students of the meaning and origin of words—debate the origin of the word "opossum." Some authorities claim it is the Algonquian word for "white animal." Other experts hold that opossum is not an American Indian word but comes from the island of Celebes where the native name for the cuscus (a tree-dwelling marsupial native to Australasia) is *o-opossuh*, meaning "little bag."

YAPOK

Because this marsupial is as much at home in the water as it is on land, it is often called the water opossum. Native to the jungles of South America, it takes its name from the Oyapok River in Guiana.

The yapok's foot-long body is covered with dark, soft, water-repellent fur that is broken by transverse bands of silvery white. The bands give a marbled effect as do the facial markings. The underside is white. Yapoks do not have prehensile tails like their

Central American water opossum or yapok

tree-dwelling relatives, but their tails—which are slightly longer than the body—are naked and scaly. The hind feet are webbed.

Yapoks dive and swim with the skill of an otter as they seek the fish and other water life on which they feed. They hunt at night and sleep during the day in dens excavated in banks above the water level.

Even when a female yapok enters a stream or lake to find food, she carries her five or six young with her. How the babies breathe in the pouch underwater is a mystery, as is the source of the horrendous stench that yapoks give off from time to time.

Four-eyed opossum

Despite their common name, these opossums do not have four eyes. However, this impression is given by two white spots surrounded by black areas just above the eyes. These spots are a protective device designed to prevent predators from striking the real eyes.

Four-eyes living in Central America have crude pouches but their South American relatives have no pouch at all. Both groups are the size of a house rat and have fur almost as silky as that of a chinchilla. The color of the fur is deep brown on the back, white or yellow underneath. The basal part of the prehensile tail is furred, the rest of it is naked and brown.

Unlike most opossums, this tree-dwelling, clever bird-catcher is quick to defend itself. Because of its courage, the natives call it *zorro*, which means "fox" in Spanish. However, female four-eyes do not attack intruders that approach the globular nests of dried leaves and grass they weave in thick foliage. At the first sign of danger they hasten to carry their young to safety. The babies grasp their mother's tail with their own tails and, as a result, "usually trail behind her like a bunch of grapes and are violently buffeted about as the mother scrambles through the foliage."

WOOLLY OPOSSUM

The popular name of this marsupial is most appropriate. It is covered with dense fur which is golden-brown above (often having a purplish wash about the shoulders) and yellow-brown below. The twenty-inch tail—about twice as long as the rest of the animal—is heavily furred at the base. The rest of the tail is naked and blotched with gray and purple.

Woolly opossums have large, protuberant bright orange eyes which contract to pinpoints in bright light. This is no handicap as woolly opossums spend most of the day sleeping in leafy nests high above the ground.

Native to the woodlands of tropical South America, the woolly opossum stays in the same area for long periods. Field observation has revealed that an individual may remain in the same tree for as long as three months, eating fruit and preying on insects and lizards.

Female woolly opossums lack a pouch but have flaps of skin on either side of the nipples. When very young, the babies cling to the nipples, but when they are older they ride on their mother's back.

MOUSE OPOSSUMS

Forty closely related species of mouse opossums inhabit Central and South America from Mexico to Patagonia. Some of these species are big as rats. Others, less than two inches in length, resemble mice in appearance and coloration. As a result, mouse opossums are often called murine opossums by naturalists—murine being derived from Muridae, the family name of the true rats and mice.

The soft, silky fur of the mouse opossums—which they continuously comb with claws and teeth—differs in color from species to species. It runs from gray to tawny, golden-brown,

Female woolly opossum with young

All mouse, or murine, opossums are attractive creatures. Most of them are golden brown or brick red above, while the under surface is yellow or white. The naked prehensile tail is pink as are the hands and feet. Pictured is Marmosa murina, *a native of Central and South America.*

russet-brown, or brick red above and yellow or white below. The prehensile tail and feet are pink while the large, bulging, jet-black eyes are masked by dark facial markings.

Although one species of mouse opossums native to Trinidad lives in caves and another inhabits the tall grass of the savannahs (treeless plains) of Brazil, most mouse opossums live on the edge of woodlands or in banana plantations. During the day they sleep in nests made of green leaves or curl up in deserted birds' nests or in dead banana fronds. Occasionally, they nap in hands of half-ripe bananas which are picked and shipped to America. When the stowaways are discovered, a frantic call is made to the nearest zoo, requesting help in capturing a "vicious creature." This is because, when threatened, mouse opossums rear up on their hind legs and bare their teeth. Actually, this is rather frightening. Like all opossums they can open their jaws to an angle of almost 180 degrees. However, rearing up and gaping the jaws does not always scare away owls and other predators. But if it does, a mouse opossum may forget to close its mouth for a half-hour or more.

Mouse opossums are very active at night. They scramble over banana leaves, jump from frond to frond, and climb up vines (which they grip with the back feet) at great speed. Although mouse opossums feast on fruit as they move about, they are primarily insect eaters. Prey is held in the forepaws and nibbled with the razor-sharp teeth.

These marsupials lack pouches. The young—which vary in number from species to species—hang onto the mother's nipples until they are a month old, at which time their eyes open and they begin to eat solid food. Now they cling to their mother with their tiny feet and tails. If one of the babies loses its grip, the female noses her offspring under her so that it can grasp her fur.

Shrew opossums

Few humans have seen one of these tiny creatures. The smallest, a native of Brazil, is less than three inches long. As their popular name indicates, these opossums resemble shrews, having short legs, tails, pointed snouts, and tiny eyes.

All known species of shrew opossums are ground dwellers. Most species burrow in loose soil seeking insects. However, one species resides beside streams and hunts for food in the water, while another species makes its home in hollow trees. Actually, little has been learned about these obscure creatures beyond the fact that they do not have pouches. Shrew opossums have far more colorful fur than their normal-sized relations. It can be mottled, stippled, or washed with russet, red, or orange. In some instances, a black stripe runs along the spine.

3. Herbivorous Marsupials of Australasia

". . . the most elegant as well as curious animals discovered in modern times."

Generally speaking, one can tell what type of food a marsupial eats by looking at its teeth. Carnivorous species (meat eaters) have a great many small incisors designed to tear flesh while the foremost incisors of herbivorous species (plant eaters) are large and designed for nipping and cutting.

Zoologists originally classified marsupials into two groups depending upon the arrangement of the front teeth. They called the flesh eaters Polyprotodontia, a word they derived from the Greek for "many teeth." Diprotodontia—the name they gave to marsupial vegetarians—is formed from the Greek words "first" and "teeth."

The feet of plant-eating marsupials also differ from those of the flesh-eating marsupials. The second and third toes on the hind feet of herbivorous marsupials are joined together up to the base of the claws. Moreover, the big toe—which bears a nail rather than a claw—is opposed to the other toes, just as a man's thumb is to his fingers.

In the Australasian region where pouched animals are—as they always have been—the dominant wildlife, most marsupials

The Australian forest is one location where kangaroos can be found.

are herbivorous. But while the plant eaters all prefer the same diet, they differ greatly in their choice of habitat. Some spend time in trees, others dwell in caves. Still others make their home on the desert floor. Kangaroos, best known of all herbivorous marsupials native to Australasia, range far and wide. One species or another can be found in grassy woodlands, scrubby sand plains, dry forests, swamps, and along river flats.

KANGAROOS

On June 24, 1770, Captain James Cook made the following entry in his journal: "It was of a light colour and the full size of a grey hound and shaped in every respect like one with a long tail which it carried like a grey hound, in short I should have taken it for a wild dog, but for its walking or running in which it jumped like a hare or a deer."

There are various legends about the origin of the name kangaroo. In Winnie-the-Pooh, A. A. Milne called two of the animals in the Hundred Acre Wood Kanga and Roo.

Cook was describing the animal he had seen that morning. There are two legendary explanations of how Cook learned its name. One is that he noticed that every time one of the animals burst out of a thicket and made off at great speed, the aborigines shouted *"Kang guru!"* Cook—so the story goes—logically assumed that "kangaroo" was the animal's name. Actually, *Kang guru* means "There he goes!"

The other legend maintains that when Cook asked the natives to name the animal that "jumped like a hare or a deer," they replied, *"Kangaroo,"* which translates into "I don't understand."

As a matter of fact, the origin of the word kangaroo has never been satisfactorily explained. Nor is it a simple task to describe a kangaroo. This is because more than fifty species of marsupial herbivores of varying behavior, coloring, habitats, and size are called kangaroos. The chore is made even more difficult because these grazers and browsers—which replace the deer and antelope of other continents—are classified according to their size and shape. The largest species are called kangaroos, while certain heavy-set species are known as wallaroos and euros. The middle-sized kangaroos are referred to as pademelons and wallabies. To add to the confusion, there is no real difference between kangaroos and wallabies other than size—and there is only a slight distinction in bulk between the smallest kangaroos and the largest wallabies.

Regardless of their common name, size, or appearance, all marsupials called kangaroos belong to the family Macropodidae (long foot). All macropods have characteristics that distinguish them from other pouched animals. Their hind limbs are long in proportion to the rest of the body and are adapted to two-footed leaping, while the forelimbs are short and slender. The large, heavy tail serves as a balance when a kangaroo takes soaring broad jumps and acts as a prop when the animal is standing still or moving slowly.

Besides modifications of the legs and tail, kangaroos have evolved teeth and stomachs designed for the eating and digesting of vegetation. Their teeth are arranged so that two large scissor-like incisors at the lower front press up against a leathery pad located between the half circle formed by the upper incisors. The stomach—like that of cows and other ruminants—consists of a series of sacs where huge numbers of bacteria and protozoa carry out a preliminary digestion of bulky herbage food.

Certain authorities call the red kangaroo, the two species and numerous subspecies of the great gray kangaroo, wallaroos, and euros "large kangaroos." Other naturalists prefer to refer to them as "true kangaroos." However, both groups agree that these animals are the biggest of the macropods.

As a matter of fact, the red kangaroo is the world's largest marsupial. A mature male—popularly called "old man" or "boomer"—may be seven feet tall and weigh over two hundred pounds. Not only are red kangaroos large and powerful animals

Red kangaroo at waterhole. Largest of macropods, the red kangaroo may weigh two hundred pounds and stand over six feet tall. The female is smaller and blue-gray in color.

but also they are richly colored. The very short, dense, woolly fur of the male is wine-red on the back, the face is gray with distinct black-and-white markings on each side of the muzzle, and the throat, chest, underparts, feet, insides of arms and legs, and the underside of the tail are white.

During the mating season, a powder-like rose-red substance is excreted from the skin on the throats and chest of male red kangaroos. Because the animals smear this powder on their backs with their forepaws, both their chests and backs are brilliantly colored while they court. Without doubt this helps impress the females.

Female red kangaroos are very attractive. Australians call them "blue flyers," a nickname suggested by the soft smokey-gray color of their upper parts and their grace and speed. However, both sexes vary in color in different parts of their range. Red kangaroos are found throughout Australia, the largest number living on the semi-arid plains of the interior.

Red kangaroos are gregarious and travel in "mobs," each controlled by a "boomer" that defends his position against ambitious young males with teeth, legs, and claws. Feinting with the forearms—which can crush an opponent in a bear hug—an experienced fighter attempts to tear the throat and shoulder muscles of his foe with his teeth. Then suddenly rearing back and using his massive tail as a brace, the animal lashes out with both legs. Not only are the kicks vicious but also fur, flesh, and bone are ripped by the long claw-like nail on the middle toe of each hind leg.

If a stream or a pond is nearby, 'roos will plunge into the water up to their chests when chased by dogs. But they do not enter the water in hopes of eluding their pursuers. They wait for the dogs to swim out to them, grab their attackers in their forearms, and hold them underwater until they drown.

Although fierce fighters when battling their own kind or when cornered by a dog, red kangaroos—like all macropods— are timid creatures. The alarm thump of a startled member of a mob will send the others scattering in all directions. In their panic they may run into fences or try to go through wires that they could jump easily. A female whose pouch contains a "joey"—the popular name for a baby kangaroo—is apt to toss it beneath a bush when fleeing real or imagined danger. This increases her chances of escaping and, as soon as possible, she returns to the youngster.

At low speed large 'roos move supported alternately by a tripod composed of the front feet and tail and by the hind feet. At high speed they leap on the hind feet alone, tail swinging up and down as a counterweight to the body. Clearing twenty or more feet with each bound and reaching heights up to ten feet,

This early representation of kangaroos is more fanciful than accurate. The joey is much too mature to be dependent upon its mother for food.

they attain speeds of thirty miles an hour.

Living in areas where drought is commonplace, red kangaroos, like most large macropods, have developed the ability to withstand torrid heat and thirst. They may go without water for weeks in the dry season, getting some moisture from the vegetation they eat. However, they do lose considerable weight.

To combat heat big kangaroos pant and lick their forepaws and chests so that the evaporating saliva will cool their skin.

Meanwhile, when the temperature soars, wallaroos reduce their need for water by resting in shady places during the day. Incidentally, wallaroos often dig holes three feet deep to find water.

Although the large kangaroos can survive famine and drought, they do not give birth when food and water are in short supply. When conditions improve the number of young in a mob rapidly increases. This is because female macropods can carry an embryo in the uterus at the same time that there is a joey in the pouch. The development of the embryo is delayed until the first joey leaves the pouch. When the pouch is permanently vacated, the second joey is born.

Red kangaroo babies remain in the pouch for approximately seven months. As indicated, a joey weighs a fraction of an ounce at birth; when it leaves the pouch it weighs between five and nine pounds. Incidentally, kangaroos rarely have twins or triplets.

Because the great gray kangaroo inhabits woodlands it is known as a "forester" in both Australia and Tasmania. It too lives in mobs led by an old man. During the day the mobs seek shelter in heavy scrub where their silvery-gray fur blends into the vegetation. Late in the evening and early in the morning, grays leave their resting places to graze in grassy clearings.

As its name indicates, this marsupial's rather short fur is predominately gray although certain subspecies have gray-brown to dark-brown fur. Besides wearing different colored coats than the great gray, some subspecies are more heavily built and move more slowly than the forester. However, the noses of all gray kangaroos are covered with fur except for a thin band of bare skin around the nostrils.

The habits of gray kangaroos parallel those of the red kangaroos. Grays spend a great deal of time washing themselves in catlike fashion and grooming their fur with the clawed joined toes on the hind feet. Grays carry their joeys in the pouch for approximately six months. When the youngster is about three months old it leaves the pouch frequently to eat and play. If

Female great gray kangaroo with joey in pouch. The youngster is about nine months old and will soon leave the pouch permanently.

frightened, the baby dives headfirst into its mother's "elastic crib."

Eventually a joey becomes too large to fit comfortably in the pouch and he is roughly evicted. If the youngster attempts to climb back his mother cuffs him until he understands that he is on his own.

WALLABIES

In 1629, the Dutch ship *Batavia* was wrecked off the coast of western Australia. While awaiting rescue, the vessel's captain, Francis Pelsaert, maintained the ship's log as if he were at sea. One entry describes an animal that lived in colonies on the rocky islands where the *Batavia* had floundered. According to Pelsaert, this creature was "a species of cat" and he recorded that it was about the size of a hare, with a civet cat's head, a long tail, and very short forepaws resembling those of a monkey. "Its

A macropod is a kangaroo if the length of its hind foot is more than ten inches. This animal is a wallaby, and its hind foot is less than ten inches. There are nearly fifty different species of wallaby in Australia.

Many wallabies have descriptive names. The red-necked wallaby has distinct reddish shoulders. One of the larger wallabies, this species abounds in Australia.

two hind legs on the contrary are upwards of half an ell in length, and it walks on . . . the flat of the heavy part of the leg . . . it sits on its hind legs and clutches its food with its forepaws just like a squirrel or monkey."

Pelsaert's entry—the first authentic description of any member of the kangaroo family—is so accurate that modern zoologists have no difficulty in recognizing his "cat" as the tammar wallaby.

No group of marsupials varies more in size than the wallabies. The red-necked wallaby is six feet long from nose to tail tip, while the tammar wallaby is not much bigger than a rabbit. Both large and small wallabies live in much thicker vegetated areas than kangaroos. In fact, there is a direct relationship between a wallaby's size and its environment. The thicker the undergrowth, the smaller the species of wallaby inhabiting it.

The numerous species and subspecies of wallabies differ greatly in habits. Some species are solitary except in the breeding season. Others live in colonies. Certain species feed at night while their relatives graze in the daylight. The latter species spend the hottest part of the day in "forms"—small depressions in the ground which become deeper with constant use.

Wallabies have great speed and agility. Thanks to long hind legs designed for hopping and leaping and their ability to hide, then take off at tremendous speed and swerve from side to side, wallabies escape from hunters, wild dogs, eagles, and the fox which Europeans introduced into Australia.

The popular names of many wallabies reveal much about their appearance: pretty-face wallaby, black-gloved wallaby, black-striped wallaby, and white-footed wallaby. The characteristic face, hip, and shoulder markings of the various species along with size and coloring (wallabies are usually gray or brown) make identification of a wallaby relatively easy.

Certain wallabies have unusual physical features. Among these is a silky-furred species slightly bigger than a rabbit with long legs and feet and a whiplike furred tail. Because the tip of the tail ends in a horny projection more or less hidden by fur, this wallaby is commonly called the nail-tailed wallaby. It is also known as the "organ grinder"—when the animal is alarmed it extends its forelimbs sideways and rotates them as it leaps to safety.

As its name implies, the nocturnal hare wallaby resembles the European hare. It has pointed ears, large hind legs, long narrow feet, and a thin tail. Despite its appearance, this marsupial was named the hare wallaby because of its habit of nesting in clumps of grass and dashing out with harelike speed when disturbed. Not only are hare wallabies extremely fast but also they have

No wallaby is more agile than the rock wallaby, known as "the chamois of Australia." These marsupials leap from crag to crag without using their forelimbs.

tremendous stamina. Dr. Bernhard Grzimek, director of the famous zoo in Frankfurt, Germany, writes of a hare wallaby that jumped over the head of a man and escaped after being chased for a quarter of a mile by dogs.

Although most wallabies have rather drab fur, two species have strikingly marked coats. The well-named spectacled hare wallaby has a bright orange ring around each eye. Equally conspicuous is the banded hare wallaby. Its thick gray fur is crossed by a dozen black and white stripes.

No other wallabies are as beautifully colored as the rock wallabies. But it is almost impossible to describe their fur. Not only does it come in a wide variety of complicated color patterns but also, in some species, the coloration of the fur changes seasonally.

Rock wallabies are called the "chamois of Australia." They live among the rocks, caves, and cliffs of mountain ranges throughout the continent. Over the centuries these slender animals have developed well-padded hind feet with granular soles to prevent slipping on smooth rocks. Most species have long, thin tails which usually are bushy or tufted at the tip. When leaping from boulder to boulder or across gullies—they can span thirteen feet—rock wallabies use their tails as rudders, and when walking along narrow ledges they employ them as balancers.

Strangely enough, these residents of rocky terrain can climb trees with ease, providing the trunks are not vertical. Even more remarkable is the fact that they do not hold on with their forelegs when clambering along branches and engaging in what is best described as aerial gymnastics.

As indicated, certain small wallabies are called pademelons. They are brown or gray in color and have shorter hind limbs, ears, and tails than other wallabies. Their dentation is also slightly different.

The red-bellied pademelon is considered a nuisance by farmers and foresters, and measures have been taken to control it. A gregarious species, the red-bellied pademelon lives in communities in thick scrub and makes tunnels through the dense undergrowth to reach the open grassy places where it grazes at sunrise and dusk.

Tree kangaroos

One would no more expect to encounter an elephant at the North Pole than to see a kangaroo in a tree. Nevertheless, there are six species of tree kangaroos, two of which are native to Australia.

Zoologists have determined that tree kangaroos were once

45

A tree kangaroo uses its tail as a support when climbing and employs it as a rudder when it leaps thirty to fifty feet from a limb to the ground, landing on all fours like a cat.

ordinary kangaroos that returned to the tree-dwelling life of their ancestors many years ago. However, because tree kangaroos spend much time on the ground they are discussed here rather than in the chapter dealing with arboreal marsupials.

Tree 'roos retain the basic macropod appearance but they have developed special modifications to aid them in climbing. These include shorter and wider hind feet than other kangaroos. The feet have round pads to prevent slipping. Meanwhile, the forelimbs are not only heavier and more powerful than those of terrestrial macropods but also have larger paws bearing very strong curved claws.

Australian tree kangaroos are either gray or brown in color. They are approximately four feet long, about half of which is the tufted tail. When tree kangaroos leap thirty to fifty feet from a limb to the ground—landing, catlike, on all fours—they stretch their tails stiffly behind them and use them as rudders. Incidentally, despite their daring jumps, tree kangaroos hold onto branches with their forelegs when climbing so that they will not fall.

Although tree kangaroos' tails lack the characteristic prehensile grip of marsupial tree dwellers, their dentation is similar to that of browsing (leaf-eating) pouched animals. The teeth of all other kangaroos are modified for grazing.

Tree kangaroos pass the day sleeping in tree forks with their heads bent between their legs. At sunset they awkwardly descend to the ground by backing down and go to the nearest waterhole. After satisfying their thirst, they begin to feed on fruit, leaves, and ferns.

RAT KANGAROOS

The musky rat kangaroo has an overall length of eighteen inches, including its seven-inch tail. In contrast to its small size, this marsupial has one of the longest scientific names of any

Hated by farmers and preyed upon by foxes, rat kangaroos are vanishing from much of their former habitat.

animal—*Hypsiprymnodon moschatus*. Its common name is due to its peculiar musky odor.

Besides being noted for its scientific name and its scent, the musky rat kangaroo is recognized as the most primitive member of the kangaroo family. Its teeth, scaly tail, and the opposable toe on the hind feet provide proof of *moschatus'* opossum ancestry.

Unlike other kangaroos, musky rat kangaroos do not leap but run on all four legs. Moreover, these solitary creatures are unique in that they eat insects as well as vegetation.

Rat kangaroos make fascinating pets. This Tasmanian rat kangaroo is so tame it can be fed bread and honey by hand.

4. Arboreal Marsupials of Australasia

"With careless ease from tree to tree."

No marsupials are more fascinating than those that spend most of their lives in trees. One species no bigger than a mouse has evolved a flight membrane that enables it to parachute. Then there are monkey-like creatures whose fur changes color if they switch diets. The tree-dwelling pouched animals also include the "native bear"—whose name, borrowed from the aborigines, is known to every crossword-puzzle addict. Television viewers are very familiar with this living teddy bear because it is featured in the "commercials" of an airline. Indeed, with the possible exception of the kangaroo, no marsupial is as well known as the koala.

KOALA

The koala is about a yard long, has large bushy ears, a protuberant curved snout, beady small black eyes, and an appealing babyish expression. However, the descriptions of the koala set down by early explorers were not very accurate. For example, there are more untruths than facts in this report published in 1827: "Our coola (sloth or native bear) is about the size of an ordinary poodle dog, with shaggy dirty-coloured fur, no tail,

and claws and feet like a bear of which it forms a tolerable miniature. It climbs trees readily and feeds upon their leaves."

There are two major errors in this description. The koala is not a sloth, an animal native to South America, nor is it a bear. Koalas and bears not only differ anatomically but also bears are omnivorous while the koala's diet requirements are highly specialized. The thick, ashy-gray fur is not "dirty-coloured." In fact, the harmless koala was nearly exterminated because of the demand for its fur. In 1927, 600,000 koala skins were exported from Queensland alone!

Koalas do have claws—strong, sharp, curved ones. Two of the toes on the handlike front feet oppose the other three. As a result, Koalas have the equivalent of three fingers and two thumbs on the forepaws. Thus they can take an extremely tight

Left, Koalas are devoted but strict parents. Long after their young have matured, they carry them on their backs.

A "deer crossing"-type warning sign in Queensland, Australia

grip on a bough or trunk. But although koalas can climb any tree they feed only on the leaves of approximately a dozen species of eucalyptus during the period when the leaves produce certain oils. When the type of oil in the foliage changes, koalas seek trees manufacturing the right oils.

Because each adult koala eats between two and three pounds of vegetation daily, it takes several acres of trees to supply enough leaves to satisfy the hunger of a whole group. This, plus the fact that the koala demands a variety of eucalyptus leaves, is the reason the Australian Government forbids the exportation of koalas to any zoo except two in California. The San Diego and San Francisco zoos are the only ones outside Australia that have access to a constant supply of the proper types of eucalyptus leaves.

On the other hand, providing koalas with water poses no problem. Actually koalas rarely drink water directly. They get

Carved souvenir belt buckle shows koala in eucalyptus tree.

A delighted traveler holding a tame young koala at the Lone Pine Koala Sanctuary, Brisbane

the moisture they need from the dew on eucalyptus leaves. Indeed, the aboriginal *koala, coola,* or *kool-la* means "one who does not drink."

Koalas usually have but one baby each year although sometimes two are born. Less than an inch long at birth and not as thick as a man's finger, the youngsters stay in the pouch for about six months. By then they are fully furred and half a foot long. After leaving the pouch they scramble onto their mother's back where they ride, quickly returning to the safety of the pouch when threatened. While male koalas ignore their offspring, the females—who tote their babies for a year—are excellent parents. But they are strict. Whenever babies are naughty, "the mother turns them over her knee and spanks them on their bottoms for minutes on end with the flat of her hand, during which time their screams are soul-rending."

53

Most Phalangerids—a group of pouched animals differing greatly in size, shape, and habits—are long-tailed tree climbers. Australians ignore scientific fact and call the majority of these arboreal marsupials "possums." Their misuse of the word perpetuates an error made in 1770 by Captain James Cook, one of the first Europeans to visit the island continent. Cook saw a naked-tailed phalanger and, noting its resemblance to the New World marsupial, called the animal "opossum." Cook was an outstanding navigator but a poor naturalist. Otherwise he would have known that no Phalangerid belongs to the same family as the opossums of the Americas.

Brush-tailed possum

Nevertheless, in common speech many phalangers are "possums." None of these marsupials has more luxuriant fur than

All seven subspecies of brush-tailed possums, including the Tasmanian brush-tail pictured here, have adapted to changes in their environment and are among the most successful of marsupials.

the brush-tailed possums whose pelts range in color from glossy gray to coppery chestnut-brown or black. Because their coats are so beautiful, millions of brush-tails have been killed to satisfy the fur trade's demand for what is humorously called "Adelaide chinchilla."

All three species of brush-tails have pointed foxy faces and sturdy compact bodies supported by short legs. The well-clawed hands manipulate objects with ease. Brush-tails are one of the few phalangers that have a brush of hair extending to the end of the tail. However, under the tip is a strip devoid of fur. This makes holding onto branches easier. The extent of the bare patch varies. It is much larger on the tapering tails of short-eared brush-tails than it is on the tails of their relatives with long ears.

Incidentally, many brush-tails no longer nest in hollow trees but make their homes on house roofs. Finding a residence was never a problem for these cat-sized marsupials. It has long been their habit to settle down in rock crevices or in deserted rabbit holes when hollow trees are not available.

Ring-tailed possum

No phalanger is more slow-moving than the nocturnal ring-tailed possum which is common throughout Australia. Some species are as big as a squirrel; others are the size of a small house cat. Generally speaking, all ring-tails have rather short faces and small ears, hands, and feet. They are easily identified by the long tapering tail which is carried coiled in a ring when not being used as an extra finger or to grasp a branch. Their pelts are quite attractive, that of the striped ring-tailed possum being of particular interest. It contains green—a color rarely seen in the fur of mammals.

Although many ring-tails live in hollow trees, most build spherical nests of twigs and leaves on branches in thick vegetation. Ring-tails are very quarrelsome. The females—who usu-

Young ring-tailed possum feeding. All baby ring-tails have dark fur that takes on the coloration of their species after they leave the pouch.

ally start the fights—breed during the summer months of January and February. Several young may be born but only two survive because the pouch encloses only two nipples.

Pygmy possums

Some phalangers are mouselike in size and in appearance. Approximately six inches in length, they are commonly called pygmy possums. Their prehensile tails account for at least half the size of these minute marsupials that feed on nectar and insects.

All pygmy possums can lower their body temperatures and become torpid during periods of inclement weather or short food supply. But the activities of these tiny creatures vary from species to species. One species—the pygmy flying possum—can

An Australian stamp shows the feather-tailed glider, a pygmy possum.

glide. These aerialists are also known as feather-tailed gliders. This name comes from the row of stiff bristles on each side of the tail which give it the appearance of a feather.

The wee honey possum, frequently called by its native name of Noolbenger, has a furred tail longer than its head and body combined. But this is not its claim to fame. It is the most specialized of all the pouched animals. Over the centuries, the Noolbenger has evolved modifications of its head that enable it to draw nectar, pollen, and microscopic insects from tubular flowers in the same fashion as honey-eating birds.

Gliders

Australians call the flying phalangers either "flying squirrels" or "gliders." These marsupials are not squirrels nor do they fly. However, they do glide. They soar through the air by means of a loose membrane attached to the sides of the body between the fore and hind limbs. When the limbs are spread, the membrane becomes taut and keeps them airborne. Taking off from the top of a tall tree, a glider drops downward and outward, then swoops upward just before landing. The latter maneuver checks

First described in 1792, the glider was one of the first Australian marsupials to receive scientific classification. However, little was known of its life and habits until relatively recently.

One of the commoner "flying possums," the sugar glider superficially resembles a squirrel.

its speed and enables it to stop in an upright position. During a glide the long bushy tail is used as a rudder.

As its name implies, the greater glider is the largest flying phalanger. If the twenty-inch tail is included, it is about a yard long. A skilled pilot, the greater glider is credited with covering 1770 feet in six successive glides.

Although the sugar glider, squirrel glider, and yellow-bellied glider are about the size of a squirrel, they are considered "large gliders." In addition to their size, all three species superficially resemble squirrels.

Sugar gliders and squirrel gliders sleep all day in a nest high above the ground. Although all gliders are vicious fighters, sugar gliders live in communities composed of parents and their young of several seasons.

Insects, flower petals, nectar, and a few leaves are the favorite foods of both species. Sugar gliders also eat the sweet sap that flows from the gum of the manna gum tree. This habit is the source of the sugar glider's popular name.

The diet and ways of the yellow-bellied glider are very similar to those of its relatives, which chirp, squeal, and screech when feeding. But the yellow-bellied glider employs its "large and varied vocabulary of shrieks, gurglings, mumblings, and hissings" when looking for food as well.

Cuscus

In the eleventh century, Ali Abul Hassun Masudi, an Arab trader, reached the Indonesian Islands. While touring them, Masudi captured an animal he called *sinad*, and he recorded in his log: "It lives for seven months in its mother's belly and always goes back there to feed." Because Masudi visited Celebes, Flores, and Timor where the cuscus is plentiful, there is every reason to believe that a cuscus is what he caught.

The first Phalangerid to be described scientifically, the cuscus was assigned the latin name *Phalanger* (fingery-one). It was an

excellent choice. Like all Phalangerids the cuscus displays great manual dexterity. Moreover, like its kin, the cuscus has a firm grip on branches. This is because phalangers have hand-shaped hind feet whose clawless big toes are opposable to the rest of the foot.

A cuscus' two-foot body is more elongated than that of a domestic cat. The head is domed, the face rounded, the eyes large with vertical pupils. The prehensile tail, which is furless at the terminal end, bears rasplike scales along the under surface. Actually, the cuscus is rather monkey-like in appearance.

But cuscuses do not move like monkeys. Although they are arboreal marsupials they are not agile climbers. If forced to stir during the day—they much prefer to sleep in thick foliage or in a hollow tree—their pace resembles that of a sloth. However cuscuses are fairly active at night when seeking food. They feed mainly upon leaves and fruits but also eat small mammals and birds.

WOMBATS

Technically, the two species of wombats should not be included in this chapter. However, they are an outstanding example of how certain former tree dwellers have adjusted to life on the ground. Since leaving their former home high above the Earth, wombats have evolved modifications that enable them to excavate burrows a hundred feet or more in length, usually ending in large bark and leaf nests. Wombats' stocky bodies are set on short sturdy legs, the claws are shovel like, the tail is very short.

Slow-moving above ground, wombats move quickly under the soil. These powerful diggers excavate their tunnels lying on their sides, pushing out the loose soil with the feet. Besides their

The first written description of an Old World marsupial probably dealt with the cuscus, whose fur changes color seasonally.

The three-foot wombat excavates burrows one hundred feet or more in length. Its teeth, like those of rodents, grow continuously and are worn away and sharpened by constant use.

adaptions for burrowing, wombats have developed some rodent characteristics. Both jaws have a single pair of incisors which, like the incisors of rodents, are chisel like and grow continuously, being ground down and sharpened by constant use. Wombats are vegetarians, leaving their burrows to feed at dusk. During the day they sunbathe in shallow depressions near the entrance to their tunnels.

Wombats are solitary creatures except during the mating season. The single young is born in late spring and carried in a well-formed pouch that opens to the rear.

5. Carnivorous Marsupials of Australasia

"Nature has all kinds of models."

While no living carnivorous marsupial is as big as *Thylacoleo*, the pouched lion of prehistoric times, some are quite large. However, the majority of carnivorous marsupials are small.

THYLACINE

The thylacine, largest of present-day carnivorous marsupials, was once common in Tasmania, a large island off the southern coast of Australia. But with the settlement of the island, the thylacine abandoned its normal diet of wallabies, small marsupials, and birds and began preying on sheep and poultry. As a result, the Tasmanian Government paid a bounty for every thylacine killed. Presently, it is sponsoring expeditions to determine if the species is extinct.

A literal translation of *Thylacinus cynocephalus*, the scientific name of the thylacine, is "pouched animal with a dog's head." However, not only the head with its long, pointed muzzle and broad, rounded ears bears a resemblance to a dog. Thylacines also have tapering tails like dogs. But they cannot wag them—the tails are set rigidly in the body.

This photo of a Tasmanian wolf or thylacine, was taken in an Australian zoo about 1933. It is one of the few pictures in existence showing the animal alive.

Because of the stripes that cross its fur, the thylacine is popularly called the Tasmanian tiger or zebra wolf. It is also known as the Tasmanian wolf because of its shape, way of running on its toes, and tooth structure. But thylacines cannot run as fast as true wolves nor do they hunt in packs.

During the day the thylacine hides in a rocky lair and seeks food at night. It will trot relentlessly after its prey and, when its quarry is exhausted, make the kill with its long canine teeth.

When the hunted rather than the hunter, and hard pressed, thylacines rise on their hind legs and hop like kangaroos. They will also leap, kangaroo-like, over obstacles when pursuing game. While chasing prey, they utter a hoarse, guttural bark.

If there are mated pairs of thylacines in the remote Tasmanian wilds, they will, hopefully, assure the future of the species. But the process will be slow. Thylacines have only two to four babies a year. Until the youngsters are able to fend for themselves, they are carried by the mother in her backward-opening, shallow pouch.

TASMANIAN DEVIL

Long considered a wanton killer of sheep, the Tasmanian devil is the most ferocious looking and horrible sounding of all marsupials. Early settlers had several reasons for dubbing Australia's second-largest carnivorous marsupial a "devil." Their choice of a name was motivated by the animal's predations, wicked expression, and ability to make weird noises, including a whining growl, a snarling cough, and a low, yelling growl.

Although vicious in appearance and habits, the predatory Tasmanian devil makes an affectionate pet when captured young and reared with kindness.

Including their twelve-inch tails, Tasmanian devils are slightly less than four feet long. They are heavily built animals, the strength being centered forward while the hindquarters are weak. The legs are short, the skull massive, the neck muscular, the muzzle short and broad, and the jaws enormous.

Extremely strong for its size and a persistent hunter, the Tasmanian devil can kill sheep and small dogs. Its usual prey is small animals, birds, and reptiles. Tasmanian devils also feed on carrion and devour bones. Their favorite hunting grounds are river banks and, if threatened while patrolling one in search of food, they will slip into the water, swim under the surface for a considerable distance, and emerge in thick cover.

Nocturnal in habits—although it enjoys basking in the sun— the Tasmanian devil is a forest dweller, making its den either in hollow logs or depressions between rocks. In former times the Tasmanian devil was common on the Australian mainland but it became extinct before the arrival of the first Europeans. Today it is restricted to game preserves in Tasmania and to remote areas of that island.

Tasmanian devils mate either in March or April and the one to four young are usually born in May. After the babies become too big to fit in the female's semicircular, backward-pointing pouch, they cling to her back and are carried about. The young are very active. They particularly delight in climbing trees with vertical trunks—something their parents cannot do, although the adults can climb.

Native cats

Four species of native cats live in Australia. Because three species—the eastern native cat, the western native cat, and the little northern native cat—are widely distributed, at least one species can be found in most parts of Australia. On the other hand, the fourth species, the tiger cat, is more common in Tasmania than on the mainland.

Because the eastern native cat preys on poultry as well as wild birds, it is heartily disliked by farmers. Note the four toes on the hind legs and the lack of spots on the tail—characteristics that distinguish this species from the tiger cat.

Little northern native cats give birth to far more babies than they can nurse. As a result, only the first eight young to reach the pouch survive.

All native cats are arboreal predators, but those that live near farms find it easier to raid chicken coops than to hunt for birds in trees. The most accomplished climber of the four is the tiger cat, the largest carnivorous marsupial in Australia. It moves swiftly through the treetops, thanks to its long sharp claws and the serrated pads on the soles of its feet that keep it from slipping.

Tiger cats are larger than domesticated felines, having bodies approximately two feet long plus a nineteen-inch tail. The tiger cat is heavily built and has powerful jaws. Like most marsupials, tiger cats have a tremendous gape and can open their mouths more than 90 degrees.

Zoologists agree that the tiger cat is the most ferocious of all marsupials—"it shows a complete lack of fear in the presence of food." Because of its size, strength, and courage, a tiger cat can take rather large prey, including small wallabies and rat kangaroos.

As indicated, these fearless hunters also attack poultry. Nevertheless, they are friends of man because they prey on rats and mice. But farmers whose chicken coops are raided do not consider any predator beneficial. Besides deliberately killing native cats, man also accidently destroys them. This is because these animals lack the instinct to avoid rabbit traps.

Numbat

The banded anteater, a marsupial better known as the numbat, has far more teeth than the average mammal. But the teeth are small and degenerate because numbats eat soft food.

Although numbats dine on ants they prefer to feast on termites. They easily remove termites from the galleries these insects excavate in tree trunks. Powerful claws on the forelimbs hook termites out of cracks and rip wood to shreds. When their prey is uncovered, numbats extend their four-inch-long cylin-

Nancy the numbat, a resident of Sydney's Taronga Zoo, holds two records. Not only has she survived in captivity for seven years but also she is presently the only banded anteater living in a zoo anywhere in the world.

drical tongues, which are covered with a sticky secretion, and lap up their dinner.

Numbats inhabit woodlands, making their grass-lined nests inside hollow logs. Actually, numbats know the location of every hollow log in their territory. When alarmed by a hawk or an eagle, a numbat scurries to the nearest log. During its flight, the bushy tail is arched over the back, probably to distract the swooping predator.

Because numbats hunt in the daytime they are always on guard against possible danger. Even when lolling in the sun with their feet outstretched—a favorite winter pastime—the rustling of treetops or the snapping of a twig will cause numbats to stand on their hind legs, look around, and quickly decide whether or not to run to the nearest hollow log.

Actually, numbats would rather flee than fight. They are extremely gentle animals. If a wild numbat is held in the hand it will struggle to escape but will not bite or scratch. Nor will this shy animal—incapable of making any noise except a sniffling grunt—defend itself from dogs or cats. As a result, the numbat is becoming rare, although it once was widely spread over southwest Australia.

BANDICOOT

Twenty species of bandicoots inhabit Australia, Tasmania, and New Guinea, ranging in size from that of a rat to that of a rabbit. All have long pointed snouts—those of some species are longer than others—that may be almost tubular in shape. The complex pattern in the pelt of dark lines and light stripes varies from species to species. So does the ability to burrow. Certain bandicoots merely dig conical pits while seeking beetles and in-

Bandicoots have the teeth of flesh-eating marsupials and the feet of pouched herbivores. This is a short-nosed bandicoot, the most widely distributed species.

sect larvae. Others excavate deep burrows in which they make their dens.

Few animals are more appealing than the rabbit-earred bandicoots, affectionately called "bilbies" by Australians. They have long ears, kangaroo-like hind legs, pointed muzzles, silvery blue-gray fur, and long bushy black-and-white or all white tails.

These nocturnal carnivores feed mostly on insects but also attack rodents, particularly the rats whose ancestors reached Australia on floating logs and on ships. The most powerful diggers of all bandicoots, bilbies live in deep spiral burrows. While the sun shines they sleep sitting up with the head tucked down on the chest and the ears laid back, the rear half of the ears folded over the eyes.

Marsupial mice

There are approximately fifty species of marsupial mice. Space does not permit more than a brief mention of a few species whose physical characteristics or behavior illustrate the great diversity of these curious animals.

While certain marsupial mice are as big as a large rat, most are small. The fat-headed and narrow-headed marsupial mice— the smallest known species of pouched animals—are so tiny that they have difficulty subduing the crickets and grasshoppers on which they feed. But these mice escape predators easily. They can slip into extremely narrow cracks—their flat heads are no thicker than the depth of a fifty-cent coin.

Most marsupial mice consume their own weight in food daily. This is because they are very active and burn up a huge amount of energy. But in times of famine, dunnarts, a group of marsupial mice with long and very narrow hind feet, become sluggish and, as a result, conserve energy and require less food. Moreover, dunnarts, which live in dry areas, use their tails for food storage. When food and water are plentiful their tails be-

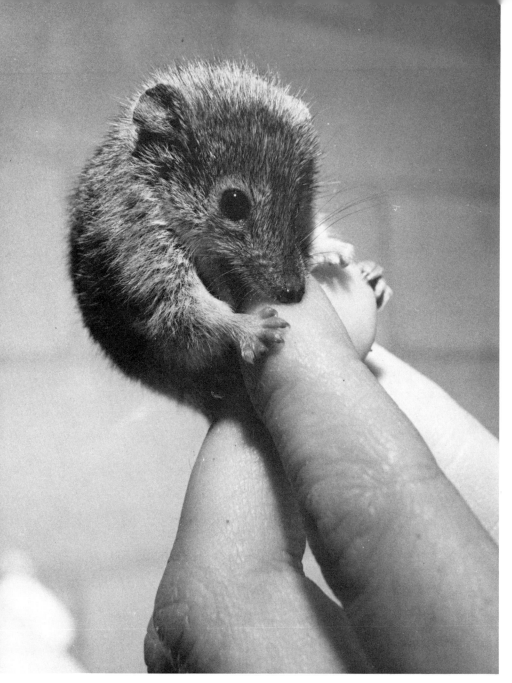

Expeditions to Australia's outback—a vast unsettled region—have discovered several new species of marsupials. This "mystery marsupial
mouse" does not have the normal dentation or blunt nose of a rodent. It
has small sharp teeth rather than large incisors and a pointed nose.

The Phascogales—brush-tailed arboreal carnivorous marsupial rats—are tree-dwelling, nocturnal hunters preying on birds, insects, and small animals. They consume so many marsupial mice they are sometimes referred to as vampire rats.

come fat and spindle shaped. During famine or drought, the tails are thin.

A number of marsupial mice are daring hunters. The crest-tailed marsupial mouse, commonly called the mulgara, is the most ferocious. Usually mulgaras stalk their prey. Like lizards they creep toward their victims with their bellies to the ground and tails lashing. Then, when close enough, they spring and make the kill. Mulgaras also imitate lizards in another way—they bask in the sun for hours. While sunning, they rest their heads on each other's backs.

Marsupial moles resemble placental moles but have more adaptions for burrowing through soil than the true moles on other continents.

Marsupial moles

These animals lack eyes and have no visible ears. But they are wondrously suited to a subterranean way of life, having a horny shield on the nose and powerful forefeet armed with strong claws for digging. Marsupial moles "swim" through soil about three inches below the surface looking for earthworms. At intervals they come to the surface for air, then "dive" back into the ground.

Like the true moles, these pouched creatures must feed constantly day and night. When their stomachs are full, they suddenly drop off to sleep, waken with a start, and feverishly renew their hunt for food.

6. The Future of Marsupials

"What of the morrow?"

On May 10, 1893, the following advertisement for furs appeared in the *Melbourne Stock and Station Journal*:

> Kangaroo, wallaby, opossum, and rabbit skins. . . .
> Opossum skins, ordinary firsts to 7s 6d,; seconds to 3 s.;
> thirds to 1s, 6d.; silver greys up to 9s. per doz.; do.
> mountain, to 18 s. per doz.

No one knows how many thousands of marsupials have been killed for their fur. Nor has an accurate count ever been made of the hordes of kangaroos whose flesh has been canned for pet food and whose hides have been made into leather.

Actually, few individuals have been concerned about the wholesale massacre of marsupials. But over the years this uncontrolled slaughter has taken a heavy toll. Formerly, mobs of a thousand red or gray kangaroos were commonplace. Today, a mob of fifty animals is considered a large one. Other species of marsupials show the same startling decrease in numbers. Fortunately, the Australian people have approved large-scale conservation activities, including the establishment of sanctu-

Little is known of the life history of the dibbler, one of Australia's rarest marsupials. Only three specimens of this nocturnal insect-eating mouse have been captured in nearly one hundred years. Due to the efforts of conservationists Down Under, the dibblers and other species may have been saved.

aries and refuges where marsupials can live undisturbed by man. These areas, called the "Last Refuges," have proved their value. When the koala was on the verge of being exterminated, a few specimens were placed in an island refuge. Living under ideal conditions and total protection, the koalas prospered and their numbers increased, enabling the authorities to restock the mainland.

Meanwhile sensible measures have been established to regulate the kangaroo problem. Hundreds of small land owners have voluntarily "posted" their property, and the International Union for the Conservation of Nature and Natural Resources has provided assistance in preserving species threatened with extinction.

It may well be that field naturalists working in the rugged interior of Australia may collect certain marsupials now thought to be extinct. But even if no remarkable discovery is made, Australians have good reason to be proud. Thanks to their efforts, their great-grandchildren will not have to look in a book or go to a zoo in order to see a numbat digging termites out of a log, a koala in a eucalyptus tree, or a joey peering out of its mother's pouch.

Index

79